CISCO CERTIFIED NET

CCNA

200-301

TOP-NOTCH QUESTIONS
FINAL PREPARATION FOR CCNA CERTIFICATION

ALVIN STOCKHARED

CISCO CERTIFIED NETWORK ASSOCIATE

SectIons:

1. Network Fundamentals

2. Network Access

3. IP Connectivity

4. IP Services

5. Security Fundamentals

6. Automation and Programmability

QUESTION 1

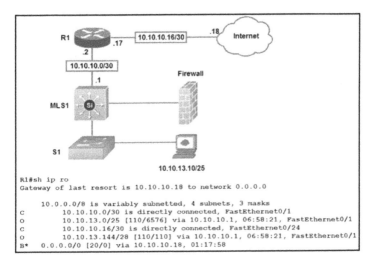

```
R1#sh ip ro
Gateway of last resort is 10.10.10.18 to network 0.0.0.0

     10.0.0.0/8 is variably subnetted, 4 subnets, 3 masks
C       10.10.10.0/30 is directly connected, FastEthernet0/1
O       10.10.13.0/25 [110/6576] via 10.10.10.1, 06:58:21, FastEthernet0/1
C       10.10.10.16/30 is directly connected, FastEthernet0/24
O       10.10.13.144/28 [110/110] via 10.10.10.1, 06:58:21, FastEthernet0/1
B*   0.0.0.0/0 [20/0] via 10.10.10.18, 01:17:58
```

Refer to the exhibit. Which type of route does R1 use to reach host 10.10.13.10/32?

    A. default route
    B. network route
    C. host route
    D. floating static route

Correct Answer: B

Section: Network Fundamentals

2

QUESTION 2

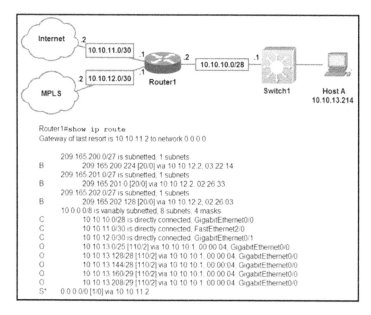

Refer to the exhibit. Which prefix does Router1 use for traffic to Host A?

    A.   10.10.10.0/28
    B.   10.10.13.0/25
    C.   10.10.13.144/28
    D.   10.10.13.208/29

Correct Answer: D

<u>Section:</u> Network Fundamentals

QUESTION 3

Drag and drop the descriptions of file-transfer protocols from the left onto the correct protocols on the right.

Select and Place:

Answer Area

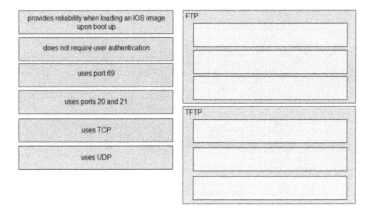

Left Items	FTP / TFTP
provides reliability when loading an IOS image upon boot up	
does not require user authentication	
uses port 69	
uses ports 20 and 21	
uses TCP	
uses UDP	

4

Correct Answer:

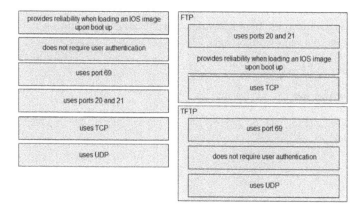

Section: Network Fundamentals

QUESTION 4

A frame that enters a switch fails the Frame Check Sequence. Which two interface counters are incremented? (Choose two.)

    A.   input errors
    B.   frame
    C.   giants
    D.   CRC
    E.   runts

Correct Answer: AD

Section: Network Fundamentals

QUESTION 5

DRAG DROP

Drag and drop the IPv4 network subnets from the left onto the correct usable host ranges on the right.

Select and Place:

Answer Area

| 172.28.228.144/18 |
| 172.28.228.144/21 |
| 172.28.228.144/23 |
| 172.28.228.144/25 |
| 172.28.228.144/29 |

| 172.28.228.1 - 172.28.229.254 |
| 172.28.224.1 - 172.28.231.254 |
| 172.28.228.129 - 172.28.228.254 |
| 172.28.228.145 - 172.28.228.150 |
| 172.28.192.1 - 172.28.255.254 |

Correct Answer:

Answer Area

| 172.28.228.144/18 |
| 172.28.228.144/21 |
| 172.28.228.144/23 |
| 172.28.228.144/25 |
| 172.28.228.144/29 |

| 172.28.228.144/23 |
| 172.28.228.144/21 |
| 172.28.228.144/25 |
| 172.28.228.144/29 |
| 172.28.228.144/18 |

Section: Network Fundamentals

6

QUESTION 6

How do TCP and UDP differ in the way that they establish a connection between two endpoints?

- A. TCP uses the three-way handshake, and UDP does not guarantee message delivery.
- B. TCP uses synchronization packets, and UDP uses acknowledgment packets.
- C. UDP provides reliable message transfer, and TCP is a connectionless protocol.
- D. UDP uses SYN, SYN ACK, and FIN bits in the frame header while TCP uses SYN, SYN ACK, and ACK bits.

Correct Answer: A

Section: Network Fundamentals

QUESTION 7

Which 802.11 frame type is association response?

- A. management
- B. protected frame
- C. action
- D. control

Correct Answer: A

Section: Network Fundamentals

Reference: https://en.wikipedia.org/wiki/802.11_Frame_Types

QUESTION 8

In which way does a spine-and-leaf architecture allow for scalability in a network when additional access ports are required?

- A. A spine switch and a leaf switch can be added with redundant connections between them.
- B. A spine switch can be added with at least 40 GB uplinks.
- C. A leaf switch can be added with connections to every spine switch.
- D. A leaf switch can be added with a single connection to a core spine switch.

Correct Answer: C

Section: Network Fundamentals

QUESTION 9

Which statement identifies the functionality of virtual machines?

- A. The hypervisor communicates on Layer 3 without the need for additional resources.
- B. Each hypervisor can support a single virtual machine and a single software switch.
- C. The hypervisor can virtualize physical components including CPU, memory, and storage.
- D. Virtualized servers run most efficiently when they are physically connected to a switch that is separate from the hypervisor.

Correct Answer: C

Section: Network Fundamentals

QUESTION 10

Which command automatically generates an IPv6 address from a specified IPv6 prefix and MAC address of an interface?

    A.   ipv6 address dhcp
    B.   ipv6 address 2001:DB8:5:112::/64 eui-64
    C.   ipv6 address autoconfig
    D.   ipv6 address 2001:DB8:5:112::2/64 link-local

Correct Answer: C

Section: Network Fundamentals

QUESTION 11

When configuring IPv6 on an interface, which two IPv6 multicast groups are joined? (Choose two.)

    A.   2000::/3
    B.   2002::5
    C.   FC00::/7
    D.   FF02::1
    E.   FF02::2

Correct Answer: DE

Section: Network Fundamentals

Reference:

https://www.cisco.com/c/en/us/td/docs/ios-xml/ios/ipv6/configuration/xe-3s/ipv6-xe-36s-book/ip6-

multicast.html

QUESTION 12

DRAG DROP

```
[root@HostTest ~]# ip route
default via 192.168.1.193 dev eth1  proto static
192.168.1.0/26 dev eth1  proto kernel  scope link src 192.168.1.200  metric 1

[root@HostTime ~]# ip addr show eth1
eth1:  mtu 1500 qdisc pfifo_fast qlen 1000
   link/ether 00:0C:22:83:79:A3 brd ff:ff:ff:ff:ff:ff
   inet 192.168.1.200/26 brd 192.168.1.255 scope global eth1
   inet6 fe80::20c:29ff:fe89:79b3/64 scope link
   valid_lft forever preferred_lft forever
```

Refer to the exhibit. Drag and drop the networking parameters from the left onto the correct values on the right.

Select and Place:

default gateway		00.0C.22
host IP address		00:0C:22:83:79:A3
NIC MAC address		192.168.1.193
NIC vendor OUI		192.168.1.200
subnet mask		255.255.255.192

Correct Answer:

Answer Area

default gateway	NIC vendor OUI
host IP address	NIC MAC address
NIC MAC address	default gateway
NIC vendor OUI	host IP address
subnet mask	subnet mask

Section: Network Fundamentals

QUESTION 13

What is the default behavior of a Layer 2 switch when a frame with an unknown destination MAC address is received?

    A. The Layer 2 switch forwards the packet and adds the destination MAC address to its MAC address table.

B. The Layer 2 switch sends a copy of a packet to CPU for destination MAC address learning.
C. The Layer 2 switch floods packets to all ports except the receiving port in the given VLAN.
D. The Layer 2 switch drops the received frame.

Correct Answer: C

<u>Section:</u> Network Fundamentals

QUESTION 14

An engineer must configure a /30 subnet between two routes. Which usable IP address and subnet mask combination meets this criteria?

A.
interface e0/0
description to XX-AXXX:XXXXX
ip address 10.2.1.3 255.255.255.252
B.
interface e0/0
description to XX-AXXX:XXXXX
ip address 192.168.1.1 255.255.255.248
C.
interface e0/0
description to XX-AXXX:XXXXX
ip address 172.16.1.4 255.255.255.248

D.
interface e0/0
description to XX-AXXX:XXXXX
ip address 209.165.201.2 225.255.255.252

Correct Answer: D

Section: Network Fundamentals

QUESTION 15

Which network allows devices to communicate without the need to access the Internet?

- A.   A. 172.9.0.0/16
- B.   B. 172.28.0.0/16
- C.   C. 192.0.0.0/8
- D.   D. 209.165.201.0/24

Correct Answer: B

Section: Network Fundamentals

QUESTION 16

```
Router(config)#interface GigabitEthernet 1/0/1
Router(config-if)#ip address 192.168.16.143 255.255.255.240
Bad mask /28 for address 192.168.16.143
```

Refer to the exhibit. Which statement explains the configuration error message that is received?

- A.   It belongs to a private IP address range.
- B.   The router does not support /28 mask.
- C.   It is a network IP address.
- D.   It is a broadcast IP address.

Correct Answer: D

Section: Network Fundamentals

QUESTION 17

Which IPv6 address type provides communication between subnets and cannot route on the Internet?

  A. link-local
  B. unique local
  C. multicast
  D. global unicast

Correct Answer: B

Section: Network Fundamentals

QUESTION 18

Which IPv6 address block sends packets to a group address rather than a single address?

  A. 2000::/3
  B. FC00::/7
  C. FE80::/10
  D. FF00::/8

Correct Answer: D

Section: Network Fundamentals

QUESTION 19

What are two reasons that cause late collisions to increment on an Ethernet interface? (Choose two.)

    A. when Carrier Sense Multiple Access/Collision Detection is used

    B. when one side of the connection is configured for half-duplex

    C. when the sending device waits 15 seconds before sending the frame again

    D. when a collision occurs after the 32nd byte of a frame has been transmitted

    E. when the cable length limits are exceeded

Correct Answer: AE

Section: Network Fundamentals

QUESTION 20

What is a benefit of using a Cisco Wireless LAN Controller?

    A. It eliminates the need to configure each access point individually.

    B. Central AP management requires more complex configurations.

    C. Unique SSIDs cannot use the same authentication method.

D.   It supports autonomous and lightweight APs.

Correct Answer: A

<u>Section:</u> Network Fundamentals

QUESTION 21

Which action is taken by switch port enabled for PoE power classification override?

A.   If a monitored port exceeds the maximum administrative value for power, the port is shutdown and err-disabled.

B.   When a powered device begins drawing power from a PoE switch port, a syslog message is generated.

C.   As power usage on a PoE switch port is checked, data flow to the connected device is temporarily paused.

D.   If a switch determines that a device is using less than the minimum configured power, it assumes the device has failed and disconnects it.

Correct Answer: A

<u>Section:</u> Network Fundamentals

Reference:
https://www.cisco.com/c/en/us/td/docs/switches/lan/catalyst6500/ios/12-2SX/configuration/ guide/book/power_over_ethernet.pdf

QUESTION 22

What occurs to frames during the process of frame flooding?

   A. Frames are sent to all ports, including those that are assigned to other VLANs.
   B. Frames are sent to every port on the switch that has a matching entry in MAC address table.
   C. Frames are sent to every port on the switch in the same VLAN except from the originating port.
   D. Frames are sent to every port on the switch in the same VLAN.

Correct Answer: C

<u>Section:</u> Network Fundamentals

QUESTION 23

Which function does the range of private IPv4 addresses perform?

   A. allows multiple companies to each use the same addresses without conflicts
   B. provides a direct connection for hosts from outside of the enterprise network
   C. ensures that NAT is not required to reach the Internet with private range addressing
   D. enables secure communications to the Internet for all external hosts

Correct Answer: A

<u>Section:</u> Network Fundamentals

QUESTION 24

Which action must be taken to assign a global unicast IPv6 address on an interface that is derived from the MAC address of that interface?

- A. explicitly assign a link-local address
- B. disable the EUI-64 bit process
- C. enable SLAAC on an interface
- D. configure a stateful DHCPv6 server on the network

Correct Answer: C

Section: Network Fundamentals

QUESTION 25

Several new coverage cells are required to improve the Wi-Fi network of an organization. Which two standard designs are recommended? (Choose two.)

- A. 5GHz provides increased network capacity with up to 23 nonoverlapping channels.
- B. 5GHz channel selection requires an autonomous access point.
- C. Cells that overlap one another are configured to use nonoverlapping channels.
- D. Adjacent cells with overlapping channels use a repeater access point.
- E. For maximum throughput, the WLC is configured to dynamically set adjacent access points to the channel.

Correct Answer: CE

Section: Network Fundamentals

QUESTION 26

How do TCP and UDP differ in the way they provide reliability for delivery of packets?

    A. TCP does not guarantee delivery or error checking to ensure that there is no corruption of data, UDP provides message acknowledgement and retransmits data if lost.

    B. TCP provides flow control to avoid overwhelming a receiver by sending too many packets at once, UDP sends packets to the receiver in a continuous stream without checking.

    C. TCP is a connectionless protocol that does not provide reliable delivery of data; UDP is a connection-oriented protocol that uses sequencing to provide reliable delivery.

    D. TCP uses windowing to deliver packets reliably; UDP provides reliable message transfer between hosts by establishing a three-way handshake.

Correct Answer: B

Section: Network Fundamentals

QUESTION 27

What are two differences between optical-fiber cabling and copper cabling? (Choose two.)

    A. A BNC connector is used for fiber connections

    B. The glass core component is encased in a cladding

    C. The data can pass through the cladding

    D. Light is transmitted through the core of the fiber

    E. Fiber connects to physical interfaces using RJ-45 connections

Correct Answer: BD

Section: Network Fundamentals

QUESTION 28

How does CAPWAP communicate between an access point in local mode and a WLC?

- A. The access point must not be connected to the wired network, as it would create a loop
- B. The access point must be connected to the same switch as the WLC
- C. The access point must directly connect to the WLC using a copper cable
- D. The access point has the ability to link to any switch in the network, assuming connectivity to the WLC

Correct Answer: D

Section: Network Fundamentals

QUESTION 29

Which IPv6 address block forwards packets to a multicast address rather than a unicast address?

- A. 2000::/3
- B. FC00::/7
- C. FE80::/10
- D. FF00::/12

Correct Answer: D

QUESTION 30

What is the difference regarding reliability and communication type between TCP and UDP?

    A.   TCP is reliable and is a connectionless protocol; UDP is not reliable and is a connection-oriented protocol.

    B.   TCP is not reliable and is a connectionless protocol; UDP is reliable and is a connection-oriented protocol.

    C.   TCP is not reliable and is a connection-oriented protocol; UDP is reliable and is a connectionless protocol.

    D.   TCP is reliable and is a connection-oriented protocol; UDP is not reliable and is a connectionless protocol.

Correct Answer: D

QUESTION 31

What are two descriptions of three-tier network topologies? (Choose two.)

    A.   The distribution layer runs Layer 2 and Layer 3 technologies

    B.   The network core is designed to maintain continuous connectivity when devices fail

C. The access layer manages routing between devices in different domains

D. The core layer maintains wired connections for each host

E. The core and distribution layers perform the same functions

Correct Answer: AB

<u>Section:</u> Network Fundamentals

QUESTION 32

Which type of ipv6 address is publicly routable in the same way as ipv4 public addresses?

    A. multicast

    B. unique local

    C. link-local

    D. global unicast

Correct Answer: D

<u>Section:</u> Network Fundamentals

QUESTION 33

What is the expected outcome when an EUI-64 address is generated?

    A. The interface ID is configured as a random 64-bit value

    B. The characters FE80 are inserted at the beginning of the MAC address of the interface

    C. The seventh bit of the original MAC address of the interface is inverted

D. The MAC address of the interface is used as the interface ID without modification

Correct Answer: C

<u>Section:</u> Network Fundamentals

QUESTION 34

A corporate office uses four floors in a building.

Floor 1 has 24 users.

Floor 2 has 29 users.

Floor 3 has 28 users.

Floor 4 has 22 users.

Which subnet summarizes and gives the most efficient distribution

of IP addresses for the router configuration?

A. 192.168.0.0/24 as summary and 192.168.0.0/28 for each floor
B. 192.168.0.0/23 as summary and 192.168.0.0/25 for each floor
C. 192.168.0.0/25 as summary and 192.168.0.0/27 for each floor
D. 192.168.0.0/26 as summary and 192.168.0.0/29 for each floor

Correct Answer: C

<u>Section:</u> Network Fundamentals

QUESTION 35

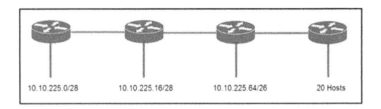

| 10.10.225.0/28 | 10.10.225.16/28 | 10.10.225.64/26 | 20 Hosts |

Refer to the exhibit. An engineer must add a subnet for a new office that will add 20 users to the network. Which IPv4 network and subnet mask combination does the engineer assign to minimize wasting addresses?

A. 10.10.225.48 255.255.255.240
B. 10.10.225.32 255.255.255.240
C. 10.10.225.48 255.255.255.224
D. 10.10.225.32 255.255.255.224

Correct Answer: D

Section: Network Fundamentals

QUESTION 36

What is a characteristic of spine-and-leaf architecture?

A. Each link between leaf switches allows for higher bandwidth.
B. It provides greater predictability on STP blocked ports.
C. It provides variable latency.
D. Each device is separated by the same number of hops.

Correct Answer: D

Section: Network Fundamentals

QUESTION 37

Which statement about Link Aggregation when implemented on a Cisco Wireless LAN Controller is true?

- A. The EtherChannel must be configured in "mode active".
- B. When enabled, the WLC bandwidth drops to 500 Mbps.
- C. To pass client traffic, two or more ports must be configured.
- D. One functional physical port is needed to pass client traffic.

Correct Answer: D

Section: Network Access

Reference:
https://www.cisco.com/c/en/us/td/docs/wireless/controller/8-2/config-guide/b_cg82/ b_cg82_chapter_010101011.html

QUESTION 38

Which two conditions must be met before SSH can operate normally on a Cisco IOS switch? (Choose two.)

- A. IP routing must be enabled on the switch.
- B. A console password must be configured on the switch.
- C. Telnet must be disabled on the switch.
- D. The switch must be running a k9 (crypto) IOS image.

E.   The ip domain-name command must be configured on the switch.

Correct Answer: DE

Section: Network Access

Reference: https://www.cisco.com/c/en/us/support/docs/security-vpn/secure-shell-ssh/4145-ssh.html

QUESTION 39

```
Atlanta#conf t
Enter configuration commands, one per line. End with CNTL/Z.
Atlanta(config)#aaa new-model
Atlanta(config)#aaa authentication login default local
Atlanta(config)#line vty 0 4
Atlanta(config-line)#login authentication default
Atlanta(config-line)#exit
Atlanta(config)#username ciscoadmin password adminadmin123
Atlanta(config)#username ciscoadmin privilege 15
Atlanta(config)#enable password cisco123
Atlanta(config)#enable secret testing1234
Atlanta(config)#end
```

Refer to the exhibit. Which password must an engineer use to enter the enable mode?

    A.   adminadmin123
    B.   cisco123
    C.   default
    D.   testing1234

Correct Answer: D

Section: Network Access

QUESTION 40

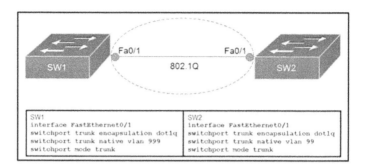

Refer to the exhibit. Which action do the switches take on the trunk link?

    A.   The trunk does not form, and the ports go into an err-disabled status.

    B.   The trunk forms, but the mismatched native VLANs are merged into a single broadcast domain.

    C.   The trunk forms, but VLAN 99 and VLAN 999 are in a shutdown state.

    D.   The trunk does not form, but VLAN 99 and VLAN 999 are allowed to traverse the link.

Correct Answer: B

<u>Section:</u> Network Access

QUESTION 41

What is the primary effect of the spanning-tree portfast command?

    A.   It immediately enables the port in the listening state.

B. It immediately puts the port into the forwarding state when the switch is reloaded.
C. It enables BPDU messages.
D. It minimizes spanning-tree convergence time.

Correct Answer: D

Section: Network Access

Reference:
https://www.cisco.com/c/en/us/td/docs/switches/lan/catalyst3560/software/release/12-2_55_se/configuration/guide/3560_scg/swstpopt.html

QUESTION 42

Which result occurs when PortFast is enabled on an interface that is connected to another switch?

    A. Root port choice and spanning tree recalculation are accelerated when a switch link goes down.
    B. After spanning tree converges, PortFast shuts down any port that receives BPDUs.
    C. VTP is allowed to propagate VLAN configuration information from switch to switch automatically.
    D. Spanning tree may fail to detect a switching loop in the network that causes broadcast storms.

Correct Answer: D

Section: Network Access

QUESTION 43

Which QoS Profile is selected in the GUI when configuring a voice over WLAN deployment?

- A. Platinum
- B. Bronze
- C. Gold
- D. Silver

Correct Answer: A

<u>Section:</u> Network Access

Reference: https://www.cisco.com/c/en/us/support/docs/wireless-mobility/wireless-lan-wlan/81831-qos-wlc-lap.html

QUESTION 44

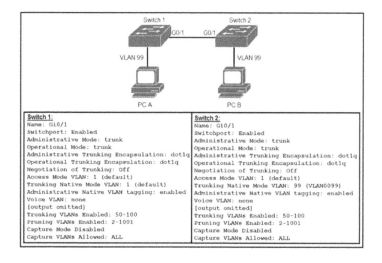

Refer to the exhibit. After the switch configuration, the ping test fails between PC A and PC B. Based on the output for switch 1, which error must be corrected?

A. The PCs are in the incorrect VLAN.
B. All VLANs are not enabled on the trunk.
C. Access mode is configured on the switch ports.
D. There is a native VLAN mismatch.

Correct Answer: D

Section: Network Access

QUESTION 45

DRAG DROP

Drag and drop the WLAN components from the left onto the correct descriptions on the right.

Select and Place:

Answer Area

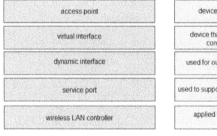

Correct Answer:

Answer Area

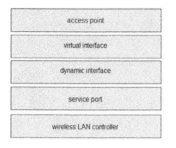
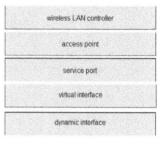

Section: Network Access

QUESTION 46

Which unified access point mode continues to serve wireless clients after losing connectivity to the Cisco Wireless LAN Controller?

- A.   local
- B.   mesh
- C.   flexconnect
- D.   sniffer

Correct Answer: C

Section: Network Access

Reference:
https://www.cisco.com/c/en/us/td/docs/wireless/controller/8-5/config-guide/b_cg85/ flexconnect.html

QUESTION 47

```
Router#
Capability Codes: R - Router, T - Trans Bridge, B - Source Route Bridge
             S -Switch, H - Host, I - IGMP, r - Repeater, P - Phone,
             D - Remote, C - CVTA, M - Two-port Mac Relay

Device ID    Local Interface Holdtime  Capability    Platform    Port ID
10.1.1.2     Gig 37/3        176              R I      CPT 600    Gig 36/41
10.1.1.2     Gig 37/1        174              R I      CPT 600    Gig 36/43
10.1.1.2     Gig 36/41       134              R I      CPT 600    Gig 37/3
10.1.1.2     Gig 36/43       134              R I      CPT 600    Gig 37/1
10.1.1.2     Ten 3/2         132              R I      CPT 600    Ten 4/2
10.1.1.2     Ten 4/2         174              R I      CPT 600    Ten 3/2
```

Refer to the exhibit. Which command provides this output?

A. show ip route
B. show cdp neighbor
C. show ip interface
D. show interface

Correct Answer: B

<u>Section:</u> Network Access

QUESTION 48

Which mode must be used to configure EtherChannel between two switches without using a negotiation protocol?

A. active
B. on
C. auto
D. desirable

Correct Answer: B

Section: Network Access

QUESTION 49

Which mode allows access points to be managed by Cisco Wireless LAN Controllers?

    A.   bridge
    B.   lightweight
    C.   mobility express
    D.   autonomous

Correct Answer: B

Section: Network Access

QUESTION 50

Which two values or settings must be entered when configuring a new WLAN in the Cisco Wireless LAN Controller GUI? (Choose two.)

    A.   QoS settings
    B.   IP address of one or more access points
    C.   SSID
    D.   profile name
    E.   management interface settings

Correct Answer: CD

Section: Network Access

QUESTION 51

Which command is used to specify the delay time in seconds for LLDP to initialize on any interface?

- A. lldp timer
- B. lldp tlv-select
- C. lldp reinit
- D. lldp holdtime

Correct Answer: C

<u>Section:</u> Network Access

Reference:
https://www.cisco.com/c/en/us/td/docs/switches/lan/catalyst2960/
software/release/12-2_37_ey/ configuration/guide/scg/swlldp.pdf

QUESTION 52

```
SW2
vtp domain cisco
vtp mode transparent
vtp password ciscotest
interface fastethernet0/1
    description connection to sw1
    switchport mode trunk
    switchport trunk encapsulation dot1q
```

Refer to the exhibit. How does SW2 interact with other switches in this VTP domain?

A. It transmits and processes VTP updates from any VTP clients on the network on its trunk ports.
B. It processes VTP updates from any VTP clients on the network on its access ports.
C. It receives updates from all VTP servers and forwards all locally configured VLANs out all trunk ports.
D. It forwards only the VTP advertisements that it receives on its trunk ports.

Correct Answer: D

Section: Network Access

Reference: https://www.cisco.com/c/en/us/support/docs/lan-switching/vtp/10558-21.html

QUESTION 53

```
SW1#sh lacp neighbor
Flags:   S - Device is requesting Slow LACPDUs
         F - Device is requesting Fast LACPDUs
         A - Device is in Active mode     P - Device is in Passive mode

Channel group 35 neighbors

Partner's information:

                 LACP port                      Admin Oper  Port    Port
Port    Flags  Priority   Dev ID         Age   key   Key    Number  State
Et1/0   SP     32768      aabb.cc80.7000  8s   0x0   0x23   0x101   0x3C
Et1/1   SP     32768      aabb.cc80.7000  8s   0x0   0x23   0x102   0x3C
```

Refer to the exhibit. Based on the LACP neighbor status, in which mode is the SW1 port channel configured?

A. mode on
B. active
C. passive
D. auto

Correct Answer: B

Section: Network Access

QUESTION 54

Two switches are connected and using Cisco Dynamic Trunking Protocol. SW1 is set to Dynamic Auto and SW2 is set to Dynamic Desirable. What is the result of this configuration?

A. The link becomes an access port.
B. The link is in an error disabled state.
C. The link is in a down state.
D. The link becomes a trunk port.

Correct Answer: D

Section: Network Access

QUESTION 55

A Cisco IP phone receives untagged data traffic from an attached PC. Which action is taken by the phone?

A. It drops the traffic.
B. It allows the traffic to pass through unchanged.
C. It tags the traffic with the native VLAN.
D. It tags the traffic with the default VLAN.

Correct Answer: B

Section: Network Access

Reference:
https://www.cisco.com/c/en/us/td/docs/switches/lan/catalyst2960x
/software/15-0_2_EX/vlan/
configuration_guide/b_vlan_152ex_2960-x_cg/b_vlan_152ex_2960-
x_cg_chapter_0110.pdf

QUESTION 56

Which design element is a best practice when deploying an 802.11b wireless infrastructure?

- A. allocating nonoverlapping channels to access points that are in close physical proximity to one another
- B. disabling TCP so that access points can negotiate signal levels with their attached wireless devices
- C. configuring access points to provide clients with a maximum of 5 Mbps
- D. setting the maximum data rate to 54 Mbps on the Cisco Wireless LAN Controller

Correct Answer: A

<u>Section:</u> Network Access

QUESTION 57

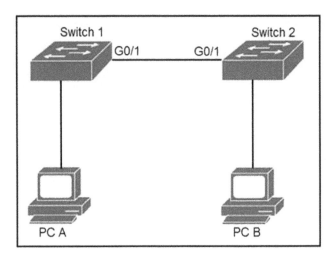

Refer to the exhibit. The network administrator wants VLAN 67 traffic to be untagged between Switch 1 and Switch 2, while all other VLANs are to remain tagged. Which command accomplishes this task?

    A.   switchport access vlan 67
    B.   switchport trunk allowed vlan 67
    C.   switchport private-vlan association host 67
    D.   switchport trunk native vlan 67

Correct Answer: D

<u>Section:</u> Network Access

QUESTION 58

Which two command sequences must be configured on a switch to establish a Layer 3 EtherChannel with an open-standard protocol? (Choose two.)

A.
interface GigabitEthernet0/0/1
channel-group 10 mode auto
B.
interface GigabitEthernet0/0/1
channel-group 10 mode on
C.
interface port-channel 10
no switchport
ip address 172.16.0.1 255.255.255.0
D.
interface GigabitEthernet0/0/1
channel-group 10 mode active
E.
interface port-channel 10
switchport
switchport mode trunk

Correct Answer: DE

Section: Network Access

QUESTION 59

```
Switch#show etherchannel summary
[output omitted]

Group     Port-channel     Protocol      Ports
--------+----------------+--------------+------------------------------
10        Po10(SU)         LACP          Gi0/0(P)      Gi0/1(P)
20        Po20(SU)         LACP          Gi0/2(P)      Gi0/3(P)
```

Refer to the exhibit. Which two commands were used to create port channel 10? (Choose two.)

> A.
> int range g0/0-1
> channel-group 10 mode active
> B.
> int range g0/0-1
> channel-group 10 mode desirable
> C.
> int range g0/0-1
> channel-group 10 mode passive
> D.
> int range g0/0-1
> channel-group 10 mode auto
> E.
> int range g0/0-1
> channel-group 10 mode on

Correct Answer: AC

Section: Network Access

QUESTION 60

```
interface GigabitEthernet3/1/4
  switchport voice vlan 50
!
```

Refer to the exhibit. An administrator is tasked with configuring a voice VLAN. What is the expected outcome when a Cisco phone is connected to the GigabitEthernet 3/1/4 port on a switch?

    A.   The phone and a workstation that is connected to the phone do not have VLAN connectivity.

    B.   The phone sends and receives data in VLAN 50, but a workstation connected to the phone sends and receives data in VLAN 1.

    C.   The phone sends and receives data in VLAN 50, but a workstation connected to the phone has no VLAN connected.

    D.   The phone and a workstation that is connected to the phone send and receive data in VLAN 50.

Correct Answer: B

Section: Network Access

QUESTION 61

```
SW1#show run int gig 0/1
interface GigabitEthernet0/1
  switchport access vlan 11
  switchport trunk allowed vlan 1-10
  switchport trunk encapsulation dot1q
  switchport trunk native vlan 5
  switchport mode trunk
  speed 1000
  duplex full
```

Refer to the exhibit. Which action is expected from SW1 when the untagged frame is received on the GigabitEthernet0/1 interface?

- A. The frame is processed in VLAN 1
- B. The frame is processed in VLAN 11
- C. The frame is processed in VLAN 5
- D. The frame is dropped

Correct Answer: C

<u>Section:</u> Network Access

QUESTION 62

```
SW1#show spanning-tree vlan 30

VLAN0030
Spanning tree enabled protocol rstp
Root ID      Priority          32798
             Address           0025.63e9.c800
             Cost              19
             Port              1 (FastEthernet 2/1)
             Hello Time        2 sec
             Max Age           30 sec
             Forward Delay     20 sec

[Output suppressed]
```

Refer to the exhibit. What two conclusions should be made about this configuration? (Choose two.)

    A. The root port is FastEthernet 2/1
    B. The designated port is FastEthernet 2/1
    C. The spanning-tree mode is PVST+
    D. This is a root bridge
    E. The spanning-tree mode is Rapid PVST+

Correct Answer: AE

Section: Network Access

QUESTION 63

A network engineer must create a diagram of a multivendor network. Which command must be configured on the Cisco devices so that the topology of the network can be mapped?

    A. Device(config)#lldp run
    B. Device(config)#cdp run

C. Device(config-if)#cdp enable
D. Device(config)#flow-sampler-map topology

Correct Answer: A

<u>Section:</u> Network Access

QUESTION 64

How do AAA operations compare regarding user identification, user services, and access control?

A. Authorization provides access control, and authentication tracks user services

B. Authentication identifies users, and accounting tracks user services

C. Accounting tracks user services, and authentication provides access control

D. Authorization identifies users, and authentication provides access control

Correct Answer: B

<u>Section:</u> Network Access

QUESTION 65

What is difference between RADIUS and TACACS+?

A. RADIUS logs all commands that are entered by the administrator, but TACACS+ logs only start, stop, and interim commands.

B. TACACS+ separates authentication and authorization, and RADIUS merges them.
C. TACACS+ encrypts only password information, and RADIUS encrypts the entire payload.
D. RADIUS is most appropriate for dial authentication, but TACACS+ can be used for multiple types of authentication.

Correct Answer: B

Section: Network Access

QUESTION 66

What is a difference between local AP mode and FlexConnect AP mode?

A. Local AP mode creates two CAPWAP tunnels per AP to the WLC
B. Local AP mode causes the AP to behave as if it were an autonomous AP
C. FlexConnect AP mode fails to function if the AP loses connectivity with the WLC
D. FlexConnect AP mode bridges the traffic from the AP to the WLC when local switching is configured

Correct Answer: D

Section: Network Access

QUESTION 67

```
R1#show ip interface brief
Interface           IP-Address     OK? Method  Status                   Protocol
FastEthernet0/0     unassigned     YES NVRAM   administratively down    down
GigabitEthernet1/0  192.168.0.1    YES NVRAM   up                       up
GigabitEthernet2/0  10.10.1.10     YES manual  up                       up
GigabitEthernet3/0  10.10.10.20    YES manual  up                       up
GigabitEthernet4/0  unassigned     YES NVRAM   administratively down    down
Loopback0           172.16.15.10   YES manual
```

Refer to the exhibit. What does router R1 use as its OSPF router-ID?

A. 10.10.1.10
B. 10.10.10.20
C. 172.16.15.10
D. 192.168.0.1

Correct Answer: C

Section: IP Connectivity

QUESTION 68

When OSPF learns multiple paths to a network, how does it select a route?

A. For each existing interface, it adds the metric from the source router to the destination to calculate the route with the lowest bandwidth.
B. It counts the number of hops between the source router and the destination to determine the route with the lowest metric.
C. It divides a reference bandwidth of 100 Mbps by the actual bandwidth of the exiting interface to calculate the route with the lowest cost.

D. It multiplies the active K values by 256 to calculate the route with the lowest metric.

Correct Answer: C

Section: IP Connectivity

QUESTION 69

When a floating static route is configured, which action ensures that the backup route is used when the primary route fails?

- A. The administrative distance must be higher on the primary route so that the backup route becomes secondary.
- B. The default-information originate command must be configured for the route to be installed into the routing table.
- C. The floating static route must have a lower administrative distance than the primary route so it is used as a backup.
- D. The floating static route must have a higher administrative distance than the primary route so it is used as a backup

Correct Answer: D

Section: IP Connectivity

QUESTION 70

```
Designated Router (ID) 10.11.11.11, Interface address 10.10.10.1
Backup Designated router (ID) 10.3.3.3, Interface address 10.10.10.3
Timer intervals configured, Hello 10, Dead 40, Wait 40, Retransmit 5
oob-resync timeout 40
Hello due in 00:00:08
Supports Link-local Signaling (LLS)
Cisco NSF helper support enabled
IETF NSF helper support enabled
Index 1/1/1, flood queue length 0
Next 0x0(0)/0x0(0)/0x0(0)
Last flood scan length is 1, maximum is 6
Last flood scan time is 0 msec, maximum is 1 msec
Neighbor Count is 3, Adjacent neighbor count is 3
Adjacent with neighbor 10.1.1.4
Adjacent with neighbor 10.2.2.2
Adjacent with neighbor 10.3.3.3 (Backup Designated Router)
Suppress hello for 0 neighbor(s)
```

Refer to the exhibit. The show ip ospf interface command has been executed on R1. How is OSPF configured?

    A.   A point-to-point network type is configured.
    B.   The interface is not participating in OSPF.
    C.   The default Hello and Dead timers are in use.
    D.   There are six OSPF neighbors on this interface.

Correct Answer: C

Section: IP Connectivity

Reference: https://www.cisco.com/c/en/us/support/docs/ip/open-shortest-path-first-ospf/13689-17.html

QUESTION 71

A user configured OSPF and advertised the Gigabit Ethernet interface in OSPF. By default, which type of OSPF network does this interface belong to?

- A. point-to-multipoint
- B. point-to-point
- C. broadcast
- D. nonbroadcast

Correct Answer: C

Section: IP Connectivity

QUESTION 72

Which attribute does a router use to select the best path when two or more different routes to the same destination exist from two different routing protocols?

- A. dual algorithm
- B. metric
- C. administrative distance
- D. hop count

Correct Answer: C

Section: IP Connectivity

QUESTION 73

Router A learns the same route from two different neighbors; one of

the neighbor routers is an OSPF neighbor, and the other is an EIGRP neighbor.

What is the administrative distance of the route that will be installed in the routing table?

    A. 20
    B. 90
    C. 110
    D. 115

Correct Answer: B

<u>Section:</u> IP Connectivity

QUESTION 74

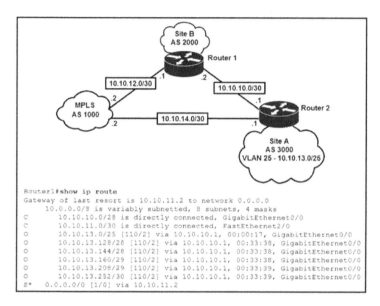

```
Router1#show ip route
Gateway of last resort is 10.10.11.2 to network 0.0.0.0
     10.0.0.0/8 is variably subnetted, 8 subnets, 4 masks
C       10.10.10.0/28 is directly connected, GigabitEthernet0/0
C       10.10.11.0/30 is directly connected, FastEthernet2/0
O       10.10.13.0/25 [110/2] via 10.10.10.1, 00:00:17, GigabitEthernet0/0
O       10.10.13.128/28 [110/2] via 10.10.10.1, 00:33:38, GigabitEthernet0/0
O       10.10.13.144/28 [110/2] via 10.10.10.1, 00:33:38, GigabitEthernet0/0
O       10.10.13.160/29 [110/2] via 10.10.10.1, 00:33:38, GigabitEthernet0/0
O       10.10.13.208/29 [110/2] via 10.10.10.1, 00:33:39, GigabitEthernet0/0
O       10.10.13.252/30 [110/2] via 10.10.10.1, 00:33:39, GigabitEthernet0/0
S*   0.0.0.0/0 [1/0] via 10.10.11.2
```

Refer to the exhibit. An engineer is bringing up a new circuit to the MPLS provider on the G10/1 interface of Router 1. The new circuit uses eBGP and learns the route to VLAN25 from the BGP path.

What is the expected behavior for the traffic flow for route 10.10.13.0/25?

A. Traffic to 10.10.13.0/25 is load balanced out of multiple interfaces.

B. Traffic to 10.10.13.0/25 is asymmetrical.

C. Route 10.10.13.0/25 is updated in the routing table as being learned from interface G10/1.

D. Route 10.10.13.0/25 learned via the G10/0 interface remains in the routing table.

Correct Answer: D

Section: IP Connectivity

QUESTION 75

Which two actions influence the EIGRP route selection process? (Choose two.)

A. The advertised distance is calculated by a downstream neighbor to inform the local router of the bandwidth on the link.
B. The router calculates the feasible distance of all paths to the destination route.
C. The router must use the advertised distance as the metric for any given route.
D. The router calculates the best backup path to the destination route and assigns it as the feasible successor.
E. The router calculates the reported distance by multiplying the delay on the exiting interface by 256.

Correct Answer: BD

Section: IP Connectivity

QUESTION 76

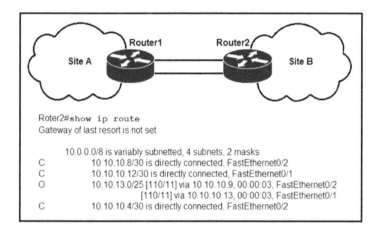

```
Roter2#show ip route
Gateway of last resort is not set

          10.0.0.0/8 is variably subnetted, 4 subnets, 2 masks
C             10.10.10.8/30 is directly connected, FastEthernet0/2
C             10.10.10.12/30 is directly connected, FastEthernet0/1
O             10.10.13.0/25 [110/11] via 10.10.10.9, 00:00:03, FastEthernet0/2
                           [110/11] via 10.10.10.13, 00:00:03, FastEthernet0/1
C             10.10.10.4/30 is directly connected, FastEthernet0/2
```

Refer to the exhibit. If OSPF is running on this network, how does Router2 handle traffic from Site B to 10.10.13.128/25 at Site A?

    A.   It sends packets out of interface Fa0/1 only.
    B.   It sends packets out of interface Fa0/2 only.
    C.   It load-balances traffic out of Fa0/1 and Fa0/2.
    D.   It cannot send packets to 10.10.13.128/25.

Correct Answer: D

Section: IP Connectivity

QUESTION 77

Which two outcomes are predictable behaviors for HSRP? (Choose two.)

A. The two routers negotiate one router as the active router and the other as the standby router.

B. The two routers share the same interface IP address, and default gateway traffic is load-balanced between them.

C. The two routers synchronize configurations to provide consistent packet forwarding.

D. Each router has a different IP address, both routers act as the default gateway on the LAN, and traffic is load-balanced between them.

E. The two routers share a virtual IP address that is used as the default gateway for devices on the LAN.

Correct Answer: AE

Section: IP Connectivity

QUESTION 78

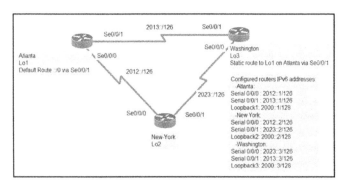

Refer to the exhibit. An engineer is configuring the New York router to reach the Lo1 interface of the Atlanta router using interface Se0/0/0 as the primary path. Which two commands must be configured on the New York router so that it can reach the Lo1 interface of the Atlanta router via Washington when the link between New York and Atlanta goes down? (Choose two.)

A. Ipv6 route 2000::1/128 2012::1
B. Ipv6 route 2000::1/128 2012::1 5
C. Ipv6 route 2000::1/128 2012::2
D. Ipv6 route 2000::1/128 2023::2 5
E. Ipv6 route 2000::1/128 2023::3 5

Correct Answer: AE

<u>Section:</u> IP Connectivity

QUESTION 79

How does HSRP provide first hop redundancy?

A. It load-balances Layer 2 traffic along the path by flooding traffic out all interfaces configured with the same VLAN.
B. It uses a shared virtual MAC and a virtual IP address to a group of routers that serve as the default gateway for hosts on a LAN.
C. It forwards multiple packets to the same destination over different routed links in the data path.
D. It load-balances traffic by assigning the same metric value to more than one route to the same destination in the IP routing table.

Correct Answer: B

<u>Section:</u> IP Connectivity

QUESTION 80

DRAG DROP

A network engineer is configuring an OSPFv2 neighbor adjacency. Drag and drop the parameters from the left onto their required categories on the right. Not all parameters are used.

Select and Place:

Answer Area

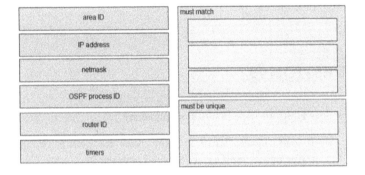

Correct Answer:

Answer Area

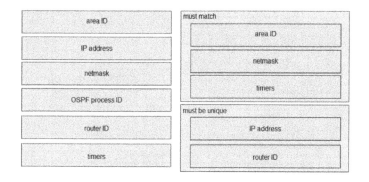

Section: IP Connectivity

QUESTION 81

R1 has learned route 192.168.12.0/24 via IS-IS, OSPF, RIP, and Internal EIGRP. Under normal operating conditions, which routing protocol is installed in the routing table?

  A. IS-IS
  B. Internal EIGRP
  C. RIP
  D. OSPF

Correct Answer: B

Section: IP Connectivity

QUESTION 82

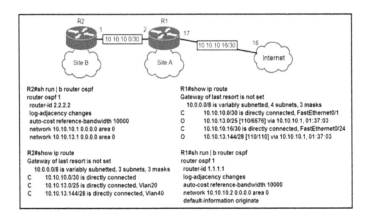

R2#sh run | b router ospf
router ospf 1
  router-id 2.2.2.2
  log-adjacency changes
  auto-cost reference-bandwidth 10000
  network 10.10.10.1 0.0.0.0 area 0
  network 10.10.13.1 0.0.0.0 area 0

R2#show ip route
Gateway of last resort is not set
  10.0.0.0/8 is variably subnetted, 3 subnets, 3 masks
C   10.10.10.0/30 is directly connected
C   10.10.13.0/25 is directly connected, Vlan20
C   10.10.13.144/28 is directly connected, Vlan40

R1#show ip route
Gateway of last resort is not set
  10.0.0.0/8 is variably subnetted, 4 subnets, 3 masks
C   10.10.10.0/30 is directly connected, FastEthernet0/1
O   10.10.13.0/25 [110/6576] via 10.10.10.1, 01:37:03
C   10.10.10.16/30 is directly connected, FastEthernet0/24
O   10.10.13.144/28 [110/110] via 10.10.10.1, 01:37:03

R1#sh run | b router ospf
router ospf 1
  router-id 1.1.1.1
  log-adjacency changes
  auto-cost reference-bandwidth 10000
  network 10.10.10.2 0.0.0.0 area 0
  default-information originate

Refer to the exhibit. The default-information originate command is configured under the R1 OSPF configuration. After testing, workstations on VLAN 20 at Site B cannot reach a DNS server on the Internet.

Which action corrects the configuration issue?

   A. Add the default-information originate command on R2.
   B. Add the always keyword to the default-information originate command on R1.
   C. Configure the ip route 0.0.0.0 0.0.0.0 10.10.10.18 command on R1.
   D. Configure the ip route 0.0.0.0 0.0.0.0 10.10.10.2 command on R2.

Correct Answer: C

<u>Section:</u> IP Connectivity

QUESTION 83

```
R1# show ip route | begin gateway
Gateway of last resort is 209.165.200.246 to network 0.0.0.0
S*  0.0.0.0/0 [1/0] via 209.165.200.246, Serial0/1/0
       is directly connected, Serial0/1/0
       172.16.0.0/16 is variably subnetted, 3 subnets, 3 masks
S      172.16.0.0/24 [1/0] via 207.165.200.250, Serial0/0/0
O      172.16.0.128/25 [110/38443] via 207.165.200.254, 00:00:23, Serial0/0/1
D      172.16.0.192/29 [90/3184439] via 207.165.200.254, 00:00:25, Serial0/0/1
       209.165.200.0/24 is variably subnetted, 4 subnets, 2 masks
C      209.165.200.248/30 is directly connected, Serial0/0/0
L      209.165.200.249/32 is directly connected, Serial0/0/0
C      209.165.200.252/30 is directly connected, Serial0/0/1
L      209.165.200.253/32 is directly connected, Serial0/0/1
```

Refer to the exhibit. With which metric was the route to host 172.16.0.202 learned?

    A. 0
    B. 110
    C. 38443
    D. 3184439

Correct Answer: C

<u>Section:</u> IP Connectivity

QUESTION 84

A user configured OSPF in a single area between two routers. A serial interface connecting R1 and R2 is running encapsulation PPP. By default, which OSPF network type is seen on this interface when the user types show ip ospf interface on R1 or R2?

    A. nonbroadcast
    B. point-to-point
    C. point-to-multipoint
    D. broadcast

QUESTION 85

Which MAC address is recognized as a VRRP virtual address?

- A. 0000.5E00.010a
- B. 0005.3709.8968
- C. 0000.0C07.AC99
- D. 0007.C070.AB01

QUESTION 86

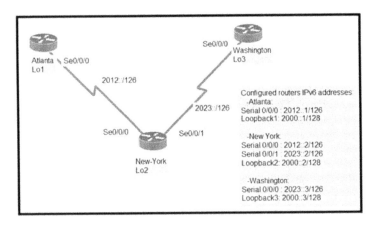

Refer to the exhibit. The New York router is configured with static routes pointing to the Atlanta and Washington sites.

Which two tasks must be performed so that the Se0/0/0 interfaces on the Atlanta and Washington routers can reach one another? (Choose two.)

- A. Configure the ipv6 route 2023::/126 2012::1 command on the Atlanta router.
- B. Configure the ipv6 route 2012::/126 2023::2 command on the Washington router.
- C. Configure the ipv6 route 2012::/126 2023::1 command on the Washington router.
- D. Configure the ipv6 route 2023::/126 2012::2 command on the Atlanta router.
- E. Configure the ipv6 route 2012::/126 s0/0/0 command on the Atlanta router.

Correct Answer: BD

Section: IP Connectivity

QUESTION 87

A router running EIGRP has learned the same route from two different paths. Which parameter does the router use to select the best path?

- A. as-path
- B. administrative distance
- C. metric
- D. cost

Correct Answer: C

Section: IP Connectivity

QUESTION 88

An engineer configured an OSPF neighbor as a designated router. Which state verifies the designated router is in the proper mode?

    A. Init
    B. 2-way
    C. Exchange
    D. Full

Correct Answer: D

Section: IP Connectivity

QUESTION 89

```
R1# show ip route

D      192.168.16.0/26 [90/2679326] via 192.168.1.1
R      192.168.16.0/24 [120/3] via 192.168.1.2
O      192.168.16.0/21 [110/2] via 192.168.1.3
i L1 192.168.16.0/27 [115/30] via 192.168.1.4
```

Refer to the exhibit. Which route does R1 select for traffic that is destined to 192.168.16.2?

    A. 192.168.16.0/21
    B. 192.168.16.0/24
    C. 192.168.26.0/26

D.   192.168.16.0/27

Correct Answer: D

<u>Section:</u> IP Connectivity

QUESTION 90

```
Gateway of last resort is 10.12.0.1 to network 0.0.0.0

O*E2 0.0.0.0/0 [110/1] via 10.12.0.1, 00:00:01, GigabitEthernet0/0
       10.0.0.0/8 is variably subnetted, 2 subnets, 2 masks
C      10.0.0.0/24 is directly connected, GigabitEthernet0/0
L      10.0.0.2/32 is directly connected, GigabitEthernet0/0
C      10.13.0.0/24 is directly connected, GigabitEthernet0/1
L      10.13.0.2/32 is directly connected, GigabitEthernet0/1
```

Refer to the exhibit. If configuring a static default route on the router
with the ip route 0.0.0.0 0.0.0.0 10.13.0.1 120 command, how does the
router respond?

A.   It starts sending traffic without a specific matching entry in
     the routing table to GigabitEthernet0/1.
B.   It immediately replaces the existing OSPF route in the routing
     table with the newly configured static route.
C.   It starts load-balancing traffic between the two default routes.
D.   It ignores the new static route until the existing OSPF default
     route is removed.

Correct Answer: D

<u>Section:</u> IP Connectivity

QUESTION 91

Refer to the exhibit. Which configuration issue is preventing the OSPF neighbor from being established between the two routers?

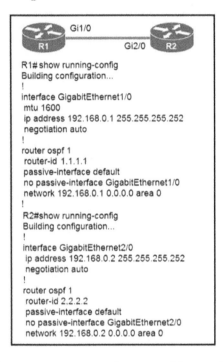

```
                Gi1/0
     R1                  Gi2/0   R2

R1# show running-config
Building configuration...
 !
interface GigabitEthernet1/0
 mtu 1600
 ip address 192.168.0.1 255.255.255.252
 negotiation auto
 !
router ospf 1
 router-id 1.1.1.1
 passive-interface default
 no passive-interface GigabitEthernet1/0
 network 192.168.0.1 0.0.0.0 area 0
 !
R2#show running-config
Building configuration...
 !
interface GigabitEthernet2/0
 ip address 192.168.0.2 255.255.255.252
 negotiation auto
 !
router ospf 1
 router-id 2.2.2.2
 passive-interface default
 no passive-interface GigabitEthernet2/0
 network 192.168.0.2 0.0.0.0 area 0
```

    A.   R1 has an incorrect network command for interface Gi1/0.
    B.   R2 should have its network command in area 1.
    C.   R1 interface Gi1/0 has a larger MTU size.
    D.   R2 is using the passive-interface default command.

Correct Answer: C

<u>Section:</u> IP Connectivity

QUESTION 92

```
R1# show ip route
....
D       172.16.32.0/27      [90/2888597172] via 20.1.1.1
O       172.16.32.0/19      [110/292094] via 20.1.1.10
R       172.16.32.0/24      [120/2] via 20.1.1.3
```

Refer to the exhibit. Router R1 is running three different routing protocols. Which route characteristic is used by the router to forward the packet that it receives for destination IP 172.16.32.1?

    A. longest prefix
    B. administrative distance
    C. cost
    D. metric

Correct Answer: A

<u>Section:</u> IP Connectivity

QUESTION 93

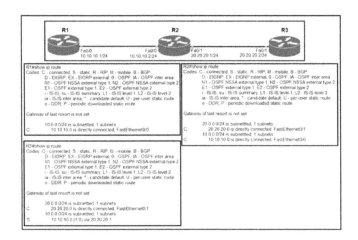

Refer to the exhibit. Router R1 Fa0/0 cannot ping router R3 Fa0/1. Which action must be taken in router R1 to help resolve the configuration issue?

A. set the default gateway as 20.20.20.2

B. configure a static route with Fa0/1 as the egress interface to reach the 20.20.2.0/24 network

C. configure a static route with 10.10.10.2 as the next hop to reach the 20.20.20.0/24 network

D. set the default network as 20.20.20.0/24

Correct Answer: C

<u>Section:</u> IP Connectivity

QUESTION 94

By default, how does EIGRP determine the metric of a route for the routing table?

    A.   It uses the bandwidth and delay values of the path to calculate the route metric.
    B.   It uses a default metric of 10 for all routes that are learned by the router.
    C.   It counts the number of hops between the receiving and destination routers and uses that value as the metric.
    D.   It uses a reference bandwidth and the actual bandwidth of the connected link to calculate the route metric.

Correct Answer: A

<u>Section:</u> IP Connectivity

QUESTION 95

Router R1 must send all traffic without a matching routing-table entry to 192.168.1.1. Which configuration accomplishes this task?

        A.
        R1#Config t
        R1(config)#ip routing
        R1(config)#ip route default-route 192.168.1.1
        B.
        R1#Config t
        R1(config)#ip routing
        R1(config)#ip route 192.168.1.1 0.0.0.0 0.0.0.0
        C.
        R1#Config t
        R1(config)#ip routing

R1(config)#ip route 0.0.0.0 0.0.0.0 192.168.1.1
D.
R1#Config t
R1(config)#ip routing
R1(config)#ip default-gateway 192.168.1.1

Correct Answer: C

Section: IP Connectivity

QUESTION 96

A packet is destined for 10.10.1.22. Which static route does the router choose to forward the packet?

   A.   ip route 10.10.1.0 255.255.255.240 10.10.255.1
   B.   ip route 10.10.1.20 255.255.255.252 10.10.255.1
   C.   ip route 10.10.1.16 255.255.255.252 10.10.255.1
   D.   ip route 10.10.1.20 255.255.255.254 10.10.255.1

Correct Answer: B

Section: IP Connectivity

QUESTION 97

```
EIGRP: 192.168.12.0/24
RIP: 192.168.12.0/27
OSPF: 192.168.12.0/28
```

Refer to the exhibit. How does the router manage traffic to 192.168.12.16?

A. It chooses the EIGRP route because it has the lowest administrative distance.
B. It load-balances traffic between all three routes.
C. It chooses the OSPF route because it has the longest prefix inclusive of the destination address.
D. It selects the RIP route because it has the longest prefix inclusive of the destination address.

Correct Answer: C

Section: IP Connectivity

QUESTION 98

What are two reasons for an engineer to configure a floating static route? (Choose two.)

A. to enable fallback static routing when the dynamic routing protocol fails
B. to route traffic differently based on the source IP of the packet
C. to automatically route traffic on a secondary path when the primary path goes down
D. to support load balancing via static routing
E. to control the return path of traffic that is sent from the router

Correct Answer: AC

Section: IP Connectivity

QUESTION 99

```
R1# show ip route

D      192.168.10.0/24      [90/2679326] via 192.168.1.1
R      192.168.10.0/27      [120/3] via 192.168.1.2
O      192.168.10.0/23      [110/2] via 192.168.1.3
i L1   192.168.10.0/13      [115/30] via 192.168.1.4
```

Refer to the exhibit. How does router R1 handle traffic to 192.168.10.16?

A. It selects the IS-IS route because it has the shortest prefix inclusive of the destination address

B. It selects the RIP route because it has the longest prefix inclusive of the destination address

C. It selects the OSPF route because it has the lowest cost

D. It selects the EIGRP route because it has the lowest administrative distance

Correct Answer: B

Section: IP Connectivity

QUESTION 100

```
IBGP route 10.0.0.0/30
RIP route 10.0.0.0/30
OSPF route 10.0.0.0/16
OSPF route 10.0.0.0/30
EIGRP route 10.0.0.1/32
```

Refer to the exhibit. A router received these five routes from different routing information sources. Which two routes does the router install in its routing table? (Choose two)

A. OSPF route 10.0.0.0/30
B. IBGP route 10.0.0.0/30
C. OSPF route 10.0.0.0/16
D. EIGRP route 10.0.0.1/32
E. RIP route 10.0.0.0/30

Correct Answer: CD

Section: IP Connectivity

QUESTION 101

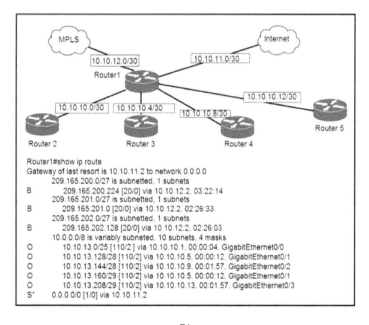

```
Router1#show ip route
Gateway of last resort is 10.10.11.2 to network 0.0.0.0
         209.165.200.0/27 is subnetted, 1 subnets
B          209.165.200.224 [20/0] via 10.10.12.2, 03:22:14
         209.165.201.0/27 is subnetted, 1 subnets
B          209.165.201.0 [20/0] via 10.10.12.2, 02:26:33
         209.165.202.0/27 is subnetted, 1 subnets
B          209.165.202.128 [20/0] via 10.10.12.2, 02:26:03
         10.0.0.0/8 is variably subneted, 10 subnets, 4 masks
O          10.10.13.0/25 [110/2 ] via 10.10.10.1, 00:00:04, GigabitEthernet0/0
O          10.10.13.128/28 [110/2] via 10.10.10.5, 00:00:12, GigabitEthernet0/1
O          10.10.13.144/28 [110/2] via 10.10.10.9, 00:01:57, GigabitEthernet0/2
O          10.10.13.160/29 [110/2] via 10.10.10.5, 00:00:12, GigabitEthernet0/1
O          10.10.13.208/29 [110/2] via 10.10.10.13, 00:01:57, GigabitEthernet0/3
S*       0.0.0.0/0 [1/0] via 10.10.11.2
```

71

Refer to the exhibit. To which device does Router1 send packets that are destined to host 10.10.13.165?

    A.   Router2
    B.   Router3
    C.   Router4
    D.   Router5

Correct Answer: B

Section: IP Connectivity

QUESTION 102

R1 has learned route 10.10.10.0/24 via numerous routing protocols. Which route is installed?

    A.   route with the next hop that has the highest IP
    B.   route with the lowest cost
    C.   route with the lowest administrative distance
    D.   route with the shortest prefix length

Correct Answer: C

Section: IP Connectivity

QUESTION 103

Which two minimum parameters must be configured on an active interface to enable OSPFV2 to operate? (Choose two.)

A.   OSPF process ID
B.   OSPF MD5 authentication key
C.   OSPF stub flag
D.   IPv6 address
E.   OSPF area

Correct Answer: AE

<u>Section:</u> IP Connectivity

QUESTION 104

R1:	SW1:	SW2:

interface Ethernet0/0
  no ip address
!
	interface Ethernet0/0
	  switchport trunk encapsulation dot1q
	  switchport mode trunk
	!
	interface Ethernet0/1
	  switchport trunk allowed vlan 10
	  switchport trunk encapsulation dot1q
	  switchport mode trunk
		interface Ethernet0/1
		  switchport trunk encapsulation dot1q
		  switchport mode trunk
		!
		interface Ethernet0/2
		  switchport access vlan 20
		  switchport mode access

Refer to the exhibit. What commands are needed to add a subinterface to Ethernet0/0 on R1 to allow for VLAN 20, with IP address 10.20.20.1/24?

> A.
> R1(config)#interface ethernet0/0
> R1(config)#encapsulation dot1q 20
> R1(config)#ip address 10.20.20.1 255.255.255.0
> B.
> R1(config)#interface   ethernet0/0.20
> R1(config)#encapsulation dot1q 20
> R1(config)#ip address 10.20.20.1 255.255.255.0
> C.
> R1(config)#interface ethernet0/0.20

R1(config)#ip address 10.20.20.1 255.255.255.0
D.
R1(config)#interface ethernet0/0
R1(config)#ip address 10.20.20.1 255.255.255.0

Correct Answer: B

Section: IP Connectivity

QUESTION 105

Which two actions are performed by the Weighted Random Early Detection mechanism? (Choose two.)

A. It supports protocol discovery.
B. It guarantees the delivery of high-priority packets.
C. It can identify different flows with a high level of granularity.
D. It can mitigate congestion by preventing the queue from filling up.
E. It drops lower-priority packets before it drops higher-priority packets.

Correct Answer: DE

Section: IP Services

QUESTION 106

```
R2#show ip nat translations
Pro  Inside global      Inside local    Outside local     Outside global
tcp  172.23.104.3:43268 10.4.4.4:43268  172.23.103.10:23  172.23.103.10:23
tcp  172.23.104.4:45507 10.4.4.5:45507  172.23.103.10:80  172.23.103.10:80
```

Refer to the exhibit. An engineer configured NAT translations and has verified that the configuration is correct. Which IP address is the source IP after the NAT has taken place?

- A. 10.4.4.4
- B. 10.4.4.5
- C. 172.23.103.10
- D. 172.23.104.4

Correct Answer: C

Section: IP Services

QUESTION 107

If a notice-level message is sent to a syslog server, which event has occurred?

- A. A network device has restarted.
- B. A debug operation is running.
- C. A routing instance has flapped.
- D. An ARP inspection has failed.

Correct Answer: C

Section: IP Services

QUESTION 108

DRAG DROP

Drag and drop the functions from the left onto the correct network components on the right.

Select and Place:

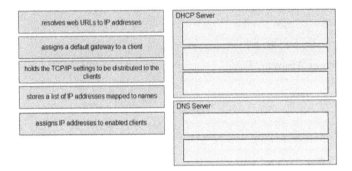

Correct Answer:

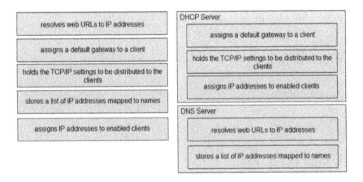

Section: IP Services

QUESTION 109

Which two tasks must be performed to configure NTP to a trusted server in client mode on a single network device? (Choose two.)

A. Enable NTP authentication.
B. Verify the time zone.
C. Specify the IP address of the NTP server.
D. Set the NTP server private key.
E. Disable NTP broadcasts.

Correct Answer: CD

Section: IP Services

QUESTION 110

DRAG DROP

Drag and drop the network protocols from the left onto the correct transport services on the right.

Select and Place:

Answer Area

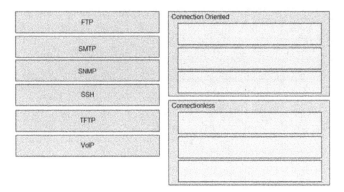

Correct Answer:

Answer Area

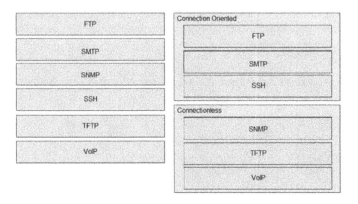

<u>Section:</u> IP Services

78

QUESTION 111

A network engineer must back up 20 network router configurations globally within a customer environment. Which protocol allows the engineer to perform this function using the Cisco IOS MIB?

- A. ARP
- B. SNMP
- C. SMTP
- D. CDP

Correct Answer: B

<u>Section:</u> IP Services

QUESTION 112

Which command enables a router to become a DHCP client?

- A. ip address dhcp
- B. ip dhcp client
- C. ip helper-address
- D. ip dhcp pool

Correct Answer: B

<u>Section:</u> IP Services

Reference: https://www.cisco.com/c/en/us/td/docs/ios-xml/ios/ipaddr_dhcp/configuration/12-4/dhcp-12-4-

book/config-dhcp-client.html

QUESTION 113

Which function does an SNMP agent perform?

    A. It sends information about MIB variables in response to requests from the NMS

    B. It manages routing between Layer 3 devices in a network

    C. It coordinates user authentication between a network device and a TACACS+ or RADIUS server

    D. It requests information from remote network nodes about catastrophic system events

Correct Answer: A

Section: IP Services

QUESTION 114

What are two roles of the Dynamic Host Configuration Protocol (DHCP)? (Choose two.)

    A. The DHCP server assigns IP addresses without requiring the client to renew them.

    B. The DHCP server leases client IP addresses dynamically.

    C. The DHCP client can request up to four DNS server addresses.

    D. The DHCP server offers the ability to exclude specific IP addresses from a pool of IP addresses.

    E. The DHCP client maintains a pool of IP addresses it can assign.

Correct Answer: BD

Section: IP Services

QUESTION 115

Which command must be entered when a device is configured as an NTP server?

    A. ntp peer
    B. ntp master
    C. ntp authenticate
    D. ntp server

Correct Answer: B

Section: IP Services

QUESTION 116

What event has occurred if a router sends a notice level message to a syslog server?

    A. A certificate has expired
    B. An interface line has changed status
    C. A TCP connection has been torn down
    D. An ICMP connection has been built

Correct Answer: B

Section: IP Services

QUESTION 117

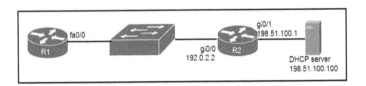

Refer to the exhibit. An engineer deploys a topology in which R1 obtains its IP configuration from DHCP. If the switch and DHCP server configurations are complete and correct.

Which two sets of commands must be configured on R1 and R2 to complete the task? (Choose two)

A.

R1(config)# interface fa0/0

R1(config-if)# ip helper-address 198.51.100.100

B.

R2(config)# interface gi0/0

R2(config-if)# ip helper-address 198.51.100.100

C.

R1(config)# interface fa0/0

R1(config-if)# ip address dhcp

R1(config-if)# no shutdown

D.

R2(config)# interface gi0/0

R2(config-if)# ip address dhcp

E.

R1(config)# interface fa0/0

R1(config-if)# ip helper-address 192.0.2.2

Correct Answer: BC

Section: IP Services

QUESTION 118

```
ip arp inspection vlan 5-10
interface fastethernet 0/1
    switchport mode access
    switchport access vlan 5
```

Refer to the exhibit. What is the effect of this configuration?

A. The switch discards all ingress ARP traffic with invalid MAC-to-IP address bindings.
B. All ARP packets are dropped by the switch.
C. Egress traffic is passed only if the destination is a DHCP server.
D. All ingress and egress traffic is dropped because the interface is untrusted.

Correct Answer: A

Section: Security Fundamentals

QUESTION 119

When a site-to-site VPN is used, which protocol is responsible for the transport of user data?

    A. IPsec
    B. IKEv1
    C. MD5
    D. IKEv2

Correct Answer: A

Section: Security Fundamentals

QUESTION 120

Which type of wireless encryption is used for WPA2 in preshared key mode?

    A. AES-128
    B. TKIP with RC4
    C. AES-256
    D. RC4

Correct Answer: C

Section: Security Fundamentals

QUESTION 121

DRAG DROP

84

Drag and drop the threat-mitigation techniques from the left onto the types of threat or attack they mitigate on the right.

Select and Place:

Answer Area

Configure BPDU guard.		802.1q double tagging
Configure dynamic ARP inspection.		ARP spoofing
Configure root guard.		unwanted superior BPDUs
Configure VACL.		unwanted BPDUs on PortFast-enabled interfaces

Correct Answer:

Answer Area

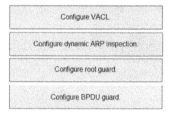

Configure BPDU guard.		Configure VACL.
Configure dynamic ARP inspection.		Configure dynamic ARP inspection.
Configure root guard.		Configure root guard.
Configure VACL.		Configure BPDU guard.

Section: Security Fundamentals

QUESTION 122

Which command prevents passwords from being stored in the configuration as plain text on a router or switch?

    A.   enable secret

B. enable password
C. service password-encryption
D. username cisco password encrypt

Correct Answer: C

<u>Section:</u> Security Fundamentals

QUESTION 123

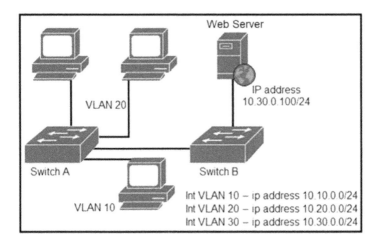

Refer to the exhibit. A network engineer must block access for all computers on VLAN 20 to the web server via HTTP. All other computers must be able to access the web server. Which configuration when applied to switch A accomplishes the task?

A. config t
   ip access-list extended wwwblock
   permit ip any any
   deny tcp any host 10.30.0.100 eq 80
   int vlan 20
   ip access-group wwwblock in

B. config t
   ip access-list extended wwwblock
   permit ip any any
   deny tcp any host 10.30.0.100 eq 80
   int vlan 30
   ip access-group wwwblock in

C. config t
   ip access-list extended wwwblock
   deny tcp any host 10.30.0.100 eq 80
   int vlan 10
   ip access-group wwwblock in

D. config t
   ip access-list extended wwwblock
   deny tcp any host 10.30.0.100 eq 80
   permit ip any any
   int vlan 20
   ip access-group wwwblock in

Correct Answer: D

Section: Security Fundamentals

QUESTION 124

```
ip arp inspection vlan 2
interface fastethernet 0/1
        switchport mode access
        switchport access vlan 2
```

Refer to the exhibit. What is the effect of this configuration?

A. The switch port remains administratively down until the interface is connected to another switch.
B. Dynamic ARP Inspection is disabled because the ARP ACL is missing.
C. The switch port interface trust state becomes untrusted.
D. The switch port remains down until it is configured to trust or untrust incoming packets.

Correct Answer: C

Section: Security Fundamentals

QUESTION 125

What is the primary difference between AAA authentication and authorization?

A. Authentication identifies and verifies a user who is attempting to access a system, and authorization controls the tasks the user can perform.
B. Authentication controls the system processes a user can access, and authorization logs the activities the user initiates.
C. Authentication verifies a username and password, and authorization handles the communication between the authentication agent and the user database.
D. Authentication identifies a user who is attempting to access a system, and authorization validates the user's password.

Correct Answer: A

Section: Security Fundamentals

QUESTION 126

When configuring a WLAN with WPA2 PSK in the Cisco Wireless LAN Controller GUI, which two formats are available to select? (Choose two.)

    A.   decimal
    B.   ASCII
    C.   hexadecimal
    D.   binary
    E.   base64

Correct Answer: BC

Section: Security Fundamentals

Reference:
https://www.cisco.com/c/en/us/td/docs/wireless/controller/7-4/configuration/guides/consolidated/
b_cg74_CONSOLIDATED/b_cg74_CONSOLIDATED_chapter_01010001.html

QUESTION 127

DRAG DROP

Drag and drop the AAA functions from the left onto the correct AAA services on the right.

Select and Place:

Answer Area

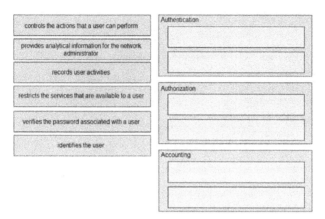

Correct Answer:

Answer Area

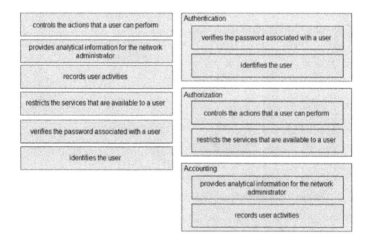

Section: Security Fundamentals

90

QUESTION 128

An engineer is asked to protect unused ports that are configured in the default VLAN on a switch. Which two steps will fulfill the request? (Choose two.)

    A.   Configure the ports as trunk ports.
    B.   Enable the Cisco Discovery Protocol.
    C.   Configure the port type as access and place in VLAN 99.
    D.   Administratively shut down the ports.
    E.   Configure the ports in an EtherChannel.

Correct Answer: CD

Section: Security Fundamentals

QUESTION 129

An email user has been lured into clicking a link in an email sent by their company's security organization.

The webpage that opens reports that it was safe, but the link could have contained malicious code.

Which type of security program is in place?

    A.   user awareness
    B.   brute force attack
    C.   physical access control
    D.   social engineering attack

Correct Answer: A

Section: Security Fundamentals

QUESTION 130

DRAG DROP

Drag and drop the Cisco Wireless LAN Controller security settings from the left onto the correct security mechanism categories on the right.

Select and Place:

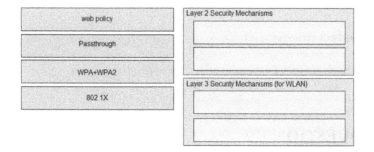

Correct Answer:

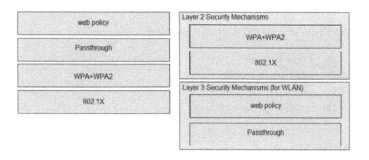

Section: Security Fundamentals

QUESTION 131

Which feature on the Cisco Wireless LAN Controller when enabled restricts management access from specific networks?

    A. TACACS
    B. CPU ACL
    C. Flex ACL
    D. RADIUS

Correct Answer: B

<u>Section:</u> Security Fundamentals

Reference: https://www.cisco.com/c/en/us/support/docs/wireless-mobility/wlan-security/71978-acl-wlc.html

QUESTION 132

Which set of actions satisfy the requirement for multifactor authentication?

    A. The user enters a user name and password, and then re-enters the credentials on a second screen.
    B. The user swipes a key fob, then clicks through an email link.
    C. The user enters a user name and password, and then clicks a notification in an authentication app on a mobile device.
    D. The user enters a PIN into an RSA token, and then enters the displayed RSA key on a login screen.

Correct Answer: C

Section: Security Fundamentals

QUESTION 133

Which configuration is needed to generate an RSA key for SSH on a router?

- A. Configure VTY access.
- B. Configure the version of SSH.
- C. Assign a DNS domain name.
- D. Create a user with a password.

Correct Answer: C

Section: Security Fundamentals

QUESTION 134

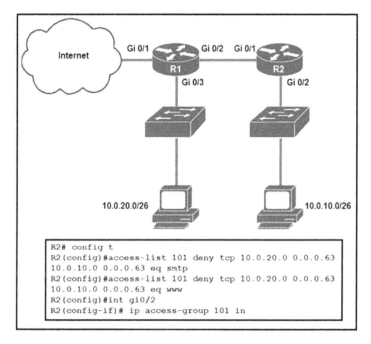

```
R2# config t
R2(config)#access-list 101 deny tcp 10.0.20.0 0.0.0.63
10.0.10.0 0.0.0.63 eq smtp
R2(config)#access-list 101 deny tcp 10.0.20.0 0.0.0.63
10.0.10.0 0.0.0.63 eq www
R2(config)#int gi0/2
R2(config-if)# ip access-group 101 in
```

Refer to the exhibit. An extended ACL has been configured and applied to router R2. The configuration failed to work as intended.

Which two changes stop outbound traffic on TCP ports 25 and 80 to 10.0.20.0/26 from the 10.0.10.0/26 subnet while still allowing all other traffic? (Choose two.)

A. Add a "permit ip any any" statement at the end of ACL 101 for allowed traffic.

B. Add a "permit ip any any" statement to the beginning of ACL 101 for allowed traffic.

C. The ACL must be moved to the Gi0/1 interface outbound on R2.

D. The source and destination IPs must be swapped in ACL 101.

E. The ACL must be configured the G10/2 interface inbound on R1.

Correct Answer: AD

Section: Security Fundamentals

QUESTION 135

An engineer must configure a WLAN using the strongest encryption type for WPA2-PSK. Which cipher fulfills the configuration requirement?

    A. WEP
    B. AES
    C. RC4
    D. TKIP

Correct Answer: B

Section: Security Fundamentals

QUESTION 136

DRAG DROP

Drag and drop the attack-mitigation techniques from the left onto the types of attack that they mitigate on the right.

Select and Place:

configure 802.1x authenticate	802.1q double-tagging VLAN-hopping attack
configure DHCP snooping	MAC flooding attack
configure the native VLAN with a nondefault VLAN ID	man-in-the-middle spoofing attack
disable DTP	switch-spoofing VLAN-hopping attack

Correct Answer:

Answer Area

configure 802.1x authenticate	configure the native VLAN with a nondefault VLAN ID
configure DHCP snooping	configure DHCP snooping
configure the native VLAN with a nondefault VLAN ID	configure 802.1x authenticate
disable DTP	disable DTP

Section: Security Fundamentals

QUESTION 137

Refer to the exhibit. What configuration on RTR-1 denies SSH access from PC-1 to any RTR-1 interface and allows all other traffic?

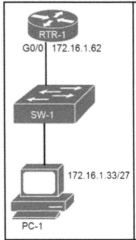

RTR-1
interface Loopback1
ip address 192.168.1.1 255.255.255.0
!
interface Loopback2
ip address 192.168.2.1 255.255.255.0
!
interface Loopback3
ip address 192.168.3.1 255.255.255.0
!
interface GigabitEthernet0/0
ip address 172.16.1.62 255.255.255.224

RTR-1
G0/0 172.16.1.62

SW-1

172.16.1.33/27

PC-1

A. access-list 100 deny tcp host 172.16.1.33 any eq 22
   access-list 100 permit ip any any

   interface GigabitEthernet0/0
   ip access-group 100 in

B. access-list 100 deny tcp host 172.16.1.33 any eq 22
   access-list 100 permit ip any any

   line vty 0 15
   access-class 100 in

C. access-list 100 deny tcp host 172.16.1.33 any eq 23
   access-list 100 permit ip any any

   interface GigabitEthernet0/0
   ip access-group 100 in

D. access-list 100 deny tcp host 172.16.1.33 any eq 23
   access-list 100 permit ip any any

   line vty 0 15
   access-class 100 in

Correct Answer: B

Section: Security Fundamentals

QUESTION 138

While examining excessive traffic on the network, it is noted that all incoming packets on an interface appear to be allowed even though an IPv4 ACL is applied to the interface. Which two misconfigurations cause this behavior? (Choose two.)

  A. The ACL is empty
  B. A matching permit statement is too broadly defined
  C. The packets fail to match any permit statement
  D. A matching deny statement is too high in the access list
  E. A matching permit statement is too high in the access list

Correct Answer: BE

Section: Security Fundamentals

QUESTION 139

The service password-encryption command is entered on a router. What is the effect of this configuration?

  A. restricts unauthorized users from viewing clear-text passwords in the running configuration
  B. prevents network administrators from configuring clear-text passwords
  C. protects the VLAN database from unauthorized PC connections on the switch

D. encrypts the password exchange when a VPN tunnel is
   established

Correct Answer: A

Section: Security Fundamentals

QUESTION 140

Which WPA3 enhancement protects against hackers viewing traffic on
the Wi-Fi network?

   A. SAE encryption
   B. TKIP encryption
   C. scrambled encryption key
   D. AES encryption

Correct Answer: A

Section: Security Fundamentals

QUESTION 141

```
ip arp inspection vlan 2-10
interface fastethernet 0/1
       ip arp inspection trust
```

Refer to the exhibit. If the network environment is operating normally,
which type of device must be connected to interface FastEthernet 0/1?

A. DHCP client
B. access point
C. router
D. PC

Correct Answer: D

Section: Security Fundamentals

QUESTION 142

```
SW1(config-line) #line vty 0 15
SW1(config-line) #no login local
SW1(config-line) #password cisco

SW2(config) #username admin1 password abcd1234
SW2(config) #username admin2 password abcd1234
SW2(config-line) #line vty 0 15
SW2(config-line) #login local

SW3(config) #username admin1 secret abcd1234
SW3(config) #username admin2 secret abcd1234
SW3(config-line) #line vty 0 15
SW3(config-line) #login local

SW4(config) #username admin1 secret abcd1234
SW4(config) #username admin2 secret abcd1234
SW4(config-line) #line console 0
SW4(config-line) #login local
```

Refer to the exhibit. An administrator configures four switches for local authentication using passwords that are stored as a cryptographic hash. The four switches must also support SSH access for administrators to manage the network infrastructure. Which switch is configured correctly to meet these requirements?

A. SW1
B. SW2
C. SW3
D. SW4

Correct Answer: C

<u>Section:</u> Security Fundamentals

QUESTION 143

Which statement correctly compares traditional networks and controller-based networks?

A. Only controller-based networks decouple the control plane and the data plane.
B. Traditional and controller-based networks abstract policies from device configurations.
C. Only traditional networks natively support centralized management.
D. Only traditional networks offer a centralized control plane.

Correct Answer: A

<u>Section:</u> Automation and Programmability

QUESTION 144

What are two benefits of network automation? (Choose two.)

A. reduced hardware footprint
B. reduced operational costs
C. faster changes with more reliable results
D. fewer network failures
E. increased network security

Correct Answer: BC

<u>Section:</u> Automation and Programmability

QUESTION 145

Which two encoding methods are supported by REST APIs? (Choose two.)

A. SGML
B. YAML
C. XML
D. JSON
E. EBCDIC

Correct Answer: CD

<u>Section:</u> Automation and Programmability

Reference:
https://www.cisco.com/c/en/us/td/docs/switches/datacenter/nexus 1000/sw/5_x/rest_api_config/

b_Cisco_N1KV_VMware_REST_API_Config_5x/

b_Cisco_N1KV_VMware_REST_API_Config_5x_chapter_010.pdf

QUESTION 146

What are two characteristics of a controller-based network? (Choose two.)

    A. It uses Telnet to report system issues.
    B. The administrator can make configuration updates from the CLI.
    C. It uses northbound and southbound APIs to communicate between architectural layers.
    D. It decentralizes the control plane, which allows each device to make its own forwarding decisions.
    E. It moves the control plane to a central point.

Correct Answer: CE

Section: Automation and Programmability

QUESTION 147

Which output displays a JSON data representation?

A.
```
{
    "response": {
    "taskId": {},
    "url": "string"
    },
    "version": "string"
}
```

B.
```
{
    "response"- {
    "taskId"- {},
    "url"- "string"
    },
    "version"- "string"
}
```

C.
```
{
    "response": {
    "taskId": {},
    "url": "string"
    },
    "version": "string"
}
```

D.
```
{
    "response", {
    "taskId", {},
    "url", "string"
    },
    "version", "string"
}
```

Correct Answer: C

<u>Section:</u> Automation and Programmability

QUESTION 148

DRAG DROP

Drag and drop the descriptions from the left onto the correct configuration-management technologies on the right.

Select and Place:

Answer Area

	Ansible
fundamental configuration elements are stored in a manifest	
uses TCP port 10002 for configuration push jobs	
uses Ruby for fundamental configuration elements	
uses SSH for remote device communication	Chef
uses TCP 8140 for communication	
uses YAML for fundamental configuration elements	Puppet

Correct Answer:

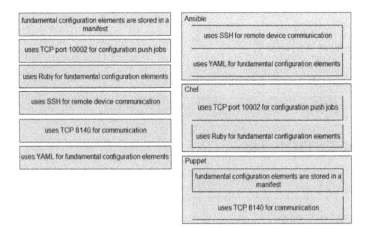

Answer Area

	Ansible
fundamental configuration elements are stored in a manifest	uses SSH for remote device communication
uses TCP port 10002 for configuration push jobs	uses YAML for fundamental configuration elements
uses Ruby for fundamental configuration elements	Chef
uses SSH for remote device communication	uses TCP port 10002 for configuration push jobs
uses TCP 8140 for communication	uses Ruby for fundamental configuration elements
uses YAML for fundamental configuration elements	Puppet
	fundamental configuration elements are stored in a manifest
	uses TCP 8140 for communication

<u>Section:</u> Automation and Programmability

QUESTION 149

Which two capabilities of Cisco DNA Center make it more extensible? (Choose two.)

    A.   REST APIs that allow for external applications to interact natively with Cisco DNA Center

    B.   adapters that support all families of Cisco IOS software

    C.   SDKs that support interaction with third-party network equipment

    D.   modular design that is upgradable as needed

    E.   customized versions for small, medium, and large enterprises

Correct Answer: AC

<u>Section:</u> Automation and Programmability

QUESTION 150

What are two southbound APIs? (Choose two.)

    A.   Thrift

    B.   DSC

    C.   CORBA

    D.   NETCONF

    E.   OpenFlow

Correct Answer: DE

<u>Section:</u> Automation and Programmability

QUESTION 151

What makes Cisco DNA Center different from traditional network management applications and their management of networks?

- A. Its modular design allows someone to implement different versions to meet the specific needs of an organization.
- B. It only supports auto-discovery of network elements in a greenfield deployment.
- C. It does not support high availability of management functions when operating in cluster mode.
- D. It abstracts policy from the actual device configuration.

Correct Answer: D

Section: Automation and Programmability

QUESTION 152

Which API is used in controller-based architectures to interact with edge devices?

- A. southbound
- B. overlay
- C. northbound
- D. underlay

Correct Answer: A

Section: Automation and Programmability

QUESTION 153

An organization has decided to start using cloud-provided services. Which cloud service allows the organization to install its own operating system on a virtual machine?

    A. platform-as-a-service
    B. network-as-a-service
    C. software-as-a-service
    D. infrastructure-as-a-service

Correct Answer: D

Section: Automation and Programmability

QUESTION 154

How do traditional campus device management and Cisco DNA Center device management differ in regards to deployment?

    A. Traditional campus device management allows a network to scale more quickly than with Cisco DNA Center device management.
    B. Cisco DNA Center device management can deploy a network more quickly than traditional campus device management.
    C. Cisco DNA Center device management can be implemented at a lower cost than most traditional campus device management options.
    D. Traditional campus device management schemes can typically deploy patches and updates more quickly than Cisco DNA Center device management.

QUESTION 155

Which purpose does a northbound API serve in a controller-based networking architecture?

A. facilitates communication between the controller and the applications
B. reports device errors to a controller
C. generates statistics for network hardware and traffic
D. communicates between the controller and the physical network hardware

QUESTION 156

What benefit does controller-based networking provide versus traditional networking?

A. allows configuration and monitoring of the network from one centralized point
B. provides an added layer of security to protect from DDoS attacks
C. combines control and data plane functionality on a single device to minimize latency

D. moves from a two-tier to a three-tier network architecture to provide maximum redundancy

Correct Answer: A

Section: Automation and Programmability

QUESTION 157

What is an advantage of Cisco DNA Center versus traditional campus device management?

A. It is designed primarily to provide network assurance.
B. It supports numerous extensibility options, including cross-domain adapters and third-party SDKs.
C. It supports high availability for management functions when operating in cluster mode.
D. It enables easy autodiscovery of network elements in a brownfield deployment.

Correct Answer: B

Section: Automation and Programmability

QUESTION 158

DRAG DROP

Drag and drop the characteristics of networking from the left onto the correct networking types on the right.

Select and Place:

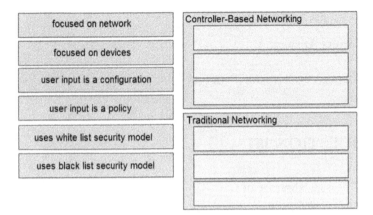

Correct Answer:

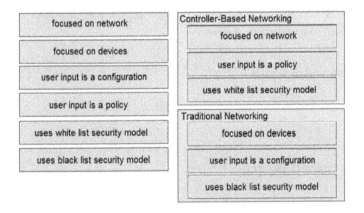

Section: Automation and Programmability

QUESTION 159

What are two fundamentals of virtualization? (Choose two.)

A. It allows logical network devices to move traffic between virtual machines and the rest of the physical network.
B. It allows multiple operating systems and applications to run independently on one physical server.
C. It allows a physical router to directly connect NICs from each virtual machine into the network.
D. It requires that some servers, virtual machines, and network gear reside on the Internet.
E. The environment must be configured with one hypervisor that serves solely as a network manager to monitor SNMP traffic.

Correct Answer: AB

Section: Automation and Programmability

QUESTION 160

How does Cisco DNA Center gather data from the network?

A. Devices use the call-home protocol to periodically send data to the controller
B. Devices establish an IPsec tunnel to exchange data with the controller
C. The Cisco CLI Analyzer tool gathers data from each licensed network device and streams it to the controller
D. Network devices use different services like SNMP, syslog, and streaming telemetry to send data to the controller

Correct Answer: D